GEOLOGY GENIUS
METAMORPHIC ROCKS

by Rebecca Pettiford

pogo

Ideas for Parents and Teachers

Pogo Books let children practice reading informational text while introducing them to nonfiction features such as headings, labels, sidebars, maps, and diagrams, as well as a table of contents, glossary, and index.

Carefully leveled text with a strong photo match offers early fluent readers the support they need to succeed.

Before Reading

- "Walk" through the book and point out the various nonfiction features. Ask the student what purpose each feature serves.
- Look at the glossary together. Read and discuss the words.

Read the Book

- Have the child read the book independently.
- Invite him or her to list questions that arise from reading.

After Reading

- Discuss the child's questions. Talk about how he or she might find answers to those questions.
- Prompt the child to think more. Ask: Metamorphic rocks are sometimes used as building materials. Have you noticed any metamorphic rocks at your school or at a park?

Pogo Books are published by Jump!
5357 Penn Avenue South
Minneapolis, MN 55419
www.jumplibrary.com

Library of Congress Cataloging-in-Publication Data

Names: Pettiford, Rebecca, author.
Title: Metamorphic rocks / by Rebecca Pettiford.
Description: Minneapolis, MN: Jump!, Inc., [2018]
Series: Geology genius | "Pogo Books are published by Jump!" | Audience: Ages 7-10.
Includes bibliographical references and index.
Identifiers: LCCN 2017059754 (print)
LCCN 2017059276 (ebook)
ISBN 9781624968389 (ebook)
ISBN 9781624968365 (hardcover: alk. paper)
ISBN 9781624968372 (pbk.)
Subjects: LCSH: Metamorphic rocks–Juvenile literature.
Metamorphism (Geology)–Juvenile literature.
Classification: LCC QE475.A2 (print) | LCC QE475.A2 P467 2018 (ebook) | DDC 552/.4—dc23
LC record available at https://lccn.loc.gov/2017059754

Editor: Kristine Spanier
Book Designer: Michelle Sonnek
Content Consultant: Sandra Feher, M.S.G.E.

Photo Credits: All photos by Shutterstock except: JTB Photo/AgeFotostock, 6–7; J-Palys/iStock, 8-9tl; Stephen Power/Alamy, 8-9tr; Hannes Magerstaedt/Stringer/Getty, 10-11; Felix Behnke/iStock, 12; John Kaprielian/Getty, 13.

Printed in the United States of America at Corporate Graphics in North Mankato, Minnesota.

TABLE OF CONTENTS

CHAPTER 1

A BIG CHANGE

Earth is made of rock. Old rock breaks down. New rock forms. This is called the **rock cycle**.

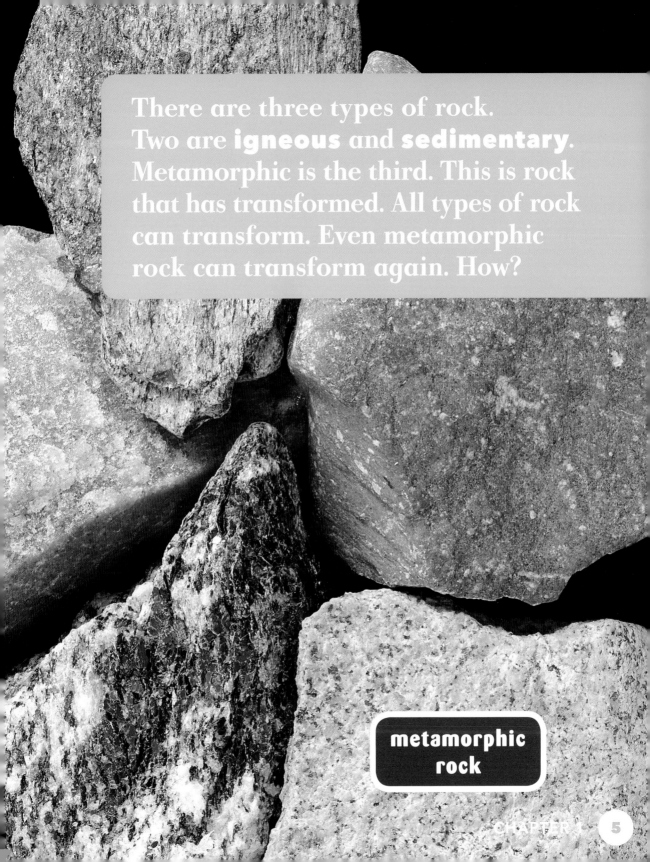

There are three types of rock. Two are **igneous** and **sedimentary**. Metamorphic is the third. This is rock that has transformed. All types of rock can transform. Even metamorphic rock can transform again. How?

metamorphic rock

Heat changes rock. So does **pressure**. New **minerals** are created. Where does the heat come from? Earth's crust is made of **plates**. They rub against each other. This makes heat. Heat also comes from **magma**. It is beneath Earth's surface. It may get into another rock. The heat bakes the rock.

TAKE A LOOK!

Heat and pressure can work alone or together to transform rock.

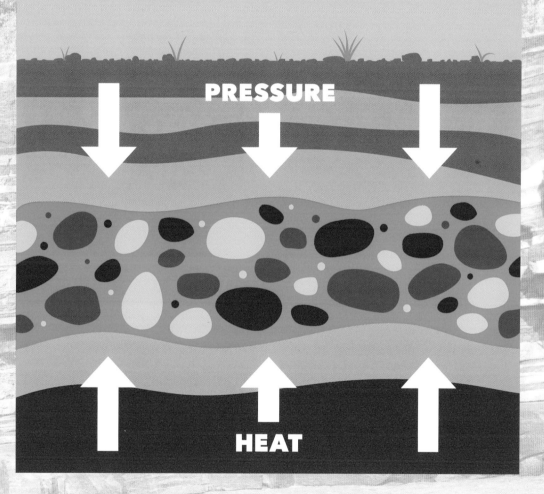

PRESSURE

HEAT

■ = igneous rock ▨ = rock layers
■ = sedimentary rock ■ = forming metamorphic rock
■ = metamorphic rock ■ = magma

lapis lazuli   FOLIATED   slate

marble   NON-FOLIATED   quartzite

There are two kinds of metamorphic rock. Foliated rock looks layered. Pressure squeezes the minerals. Non-foliated rock does not look layered. It may have had pressure from all sides. Or its minerals do not have distinctive growth patterns.

Lapis lazuli is rare. Its blue color makes it special. The people of Egypt once used it to decorate important items.

DID YOU KNOW?

King Tut was buried in a tomb. When? More than 3,300 years ago! A gold mask covered the king's mummy. It is made of lapis lazuli, quartz, and other stones.

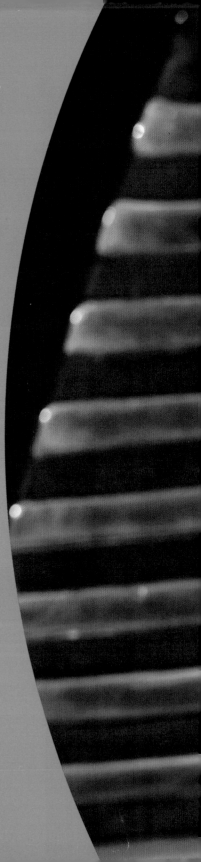

lapis lazuli

CHAPTER 2

AMAZING FORMATIONS

New York City has tall skyscrapers. What lies beneath them? **Schist** rock. It serves as a sturdy foundation.

New York City

We can see this rock. It is in the city's Central Park. It started as soft mud on a seafloor. When? More than 450 million years ago. Pressure **compressed** it. Plate collisions forced it up.

schist

Pipestone National Monument is in Minnesota. Pipestone is formed from mud layers. Heat transformed the mud over time. So did pressure. This red rock is layered with **quartzite**.

DID YOU KNOW?

Native people have **quarried** pipestone for more than 3,000 years. Why? It is soft. They carve special objects from it.

quartzite

pipestone

Matterhorn
Mountain

Matterhorn Mountain is in Europe. It rises above the Alps. How did it form? Two plates collided. The European plate is at the bottom. It is made of sedimentary rock. But the peak is from the African plate. It is made of metamorphic rock.

DID YOU KNOW?

Matterhorn formed more than 45 million years ago. The peak is older than the base.

CHAPTER 3

IN OUR DAILY LIVES

Limestone transforms into **marble**. We use it to build statues. What else? Monuments. Buildings.

You may have marble in your bathroom. Crushed marble is in some toothpastes. It helps keep our teeth clean.

marble

Slate and schist are strong. They look nice. We use them in homes. Offices. Buildings. How? We make floors. Roofs. We use them outside.

Earth has amazing rock. We still have a lot to learn from it.

DID YOU KNOW?

Earth is more than 4.5 billion years old. The oldest rock found is about 3.9 billion years old. What kind is it? Metamorphic!

slate
roof

ACTIVITIES & TOOLS

MARBLED PAPER

Marble forms when limestone is heated and compressed. Sometimes other minerals are added to it during the transformation. This creates a unique colored stone. Create paper with this marbled effect.

What You Need:
- shallow pan
- shaving cream
- food coloring, variety of colors
- spreader or plastic knife
- cardstock

❶ Fill the bottom of the pan with shaving cream.

❷ Squirt food coloring on top of the shaving cream.

❸ Use the spreader to lightly swirl the colors around.

❹ Lay your cardstock gently into the colored shaving cream. Press it down.

❺ Lift up the paper and scrape off the extra shaving cream.

❻ Allow the paper to dry.

❼ Repeat steps to make more marbled paper.

GLOSSARY

compressed: Pressed or squeezed together.

igneous: Rock made by cooled magma or lava that has hardened.

limestone: Rock formed from the remains of shells or coral.

magma: Melted rock beneath Earth's surface that becomes lava when it flows out of volcanoes and fissures.

marble: Limestone that has transformed and is used in architecture and sculpture.

minerals: Solid, natural substances with crystal structures, usually obtained from the ground.

plates: The flat, rigid, rocky pieces that make up Earth's outer crust.

pressure: The force produced by pressing on something.

quarried: To dig or take stone from a source, sometimes using sledgehammers, wedges, or picks to break past hard outer rock.

quartzite: Compact, grainy non-foliated rock made of transformed sandstone.

rock cycle: The continuous process by which rocks are created, changed from one form to another, destroyed, and then formed again.

schist: Metamorphic rock that can be split along nearly parallel planes.

sedimentary: Rock that is formed by layers of sediment that have been pressed together.

slate: Dense, fine-grained metamorphic rock formed by the compression of shale or other rock that splits into thin layers or plates.

INDEX

TO LEARN MORE

Learning more is as easy as 1, 2, 3.

1) Go to www.factsurfer.com

2) Enter "metamorphicrocks" into the search box.

3) Click the "Surf" button to see a list of websites.

With factsurfer, finding more information is just a click away.